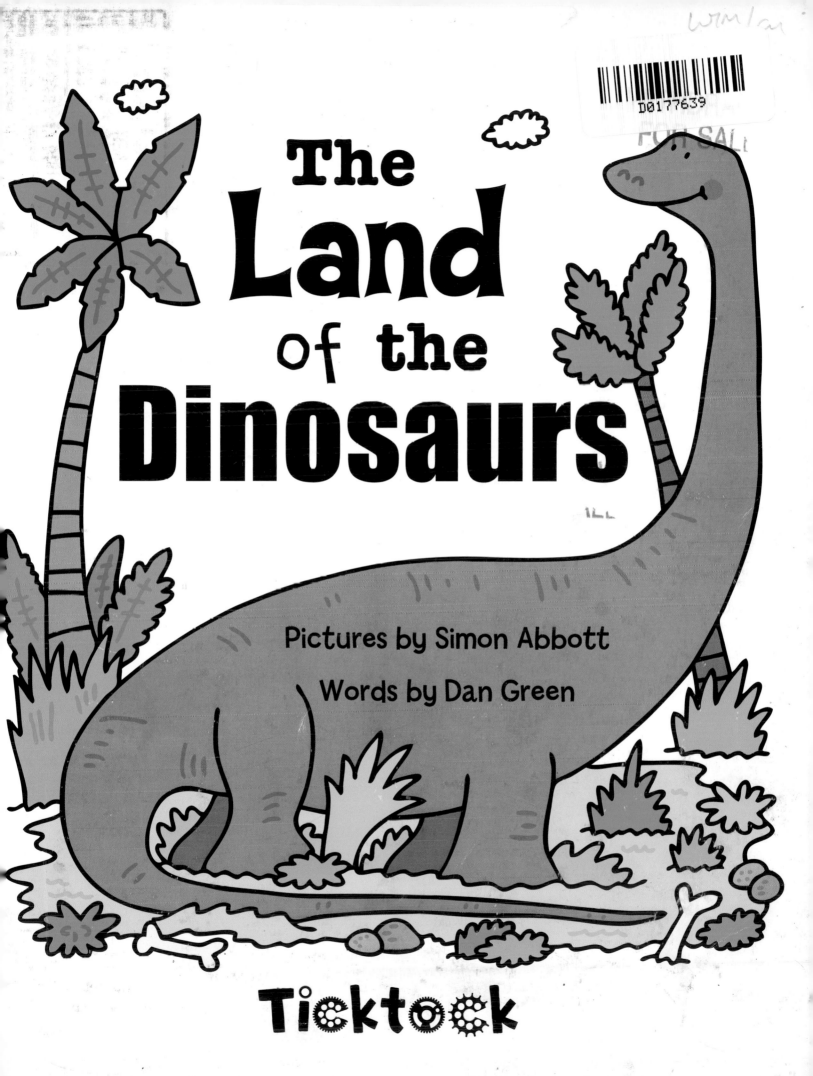

The Land of the Dinosaurs

Pictures by Simon Abbott

Words by Dan Green

Ticktock

W--rld of Din--s

Millions of years ago, dinosaurs ruled the land. Some were bloodthirsty hunters and some were peaceful plant-eaters - but all of them were mind-blowing marvels!

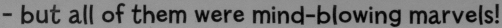

Welcome to our world!

The dinosaurs were a group of **reptiles** that now no longer live on Earth.

Dinosaurs had **four** limbs and walked on two or four legs.

Dinosaurs stood **upright** and swung their legs underneath their bodies - just like mammals do...even humans!

Scientists called **palaeontologists** (say pale-ee-on-toll-oh-gists) study fossils found in the rocks to learn about these ancient animals.

Some dinosaurs had giant **plates** or **horns** on their bodies!

FUN FACTS

Dinosaurs roamed the planet for about **165 million** years. Humans have only been around for 2-3 million years! We are closer in time to T. rex than T. rex was to the first dinosaur.

Dinosaur **teeth** give us clues about what they ate. Most meat-eating dinosaurs had large pointy teeth, but some had none at all!

Plant-eating dinosaurs had pencil-like teeth that were good for chomping on plants.

Check out my chompers!

Their skin was either **scaly** like a lizard's or covered in feathers.

All dinosaurs lived on land and laid **eggs**.

The **smallest** dino would have fit in the palm of your hand, while the most **gigantic** dino was taller than a six-storey building.

The earliest dinosaur was **Eoraptor** (say e-o-rap-tor), which lived around 230 million years ago.

WOW!

Meat Munchers

Meet the dinos that dine out on other dinos! This bunch of terrifying dino-killers loved to guzzle gristle, munch meat and tear up tendons. Rooaarr!

Oh, ha, ha! Very funny!

Carnivorous (meat-eating) dinosaurs had scary teeth and claws - just great for biting, slashing and chomping their way through tough dino-hide.

T. rex's teeth were as big as **bananas**!

Catch me if you can!

Not all meat-eaters were large. Speedy **Compsognathus** (say comp-sog-nay-thuss) was no bigger than a chicken.

Super-smart **Troodon** (say tro-uh-don) had big eyes and a large brain for planning its deadly raids.

My plan

Operation Meat Feast

....but all my socks are RUINED!

Velociraptor's (say vel-o-sir-rap-tor) big curved claws on its second toe were shaped like curved daggers and each as big as your thumb! Gulp!

Yikes!

Canny **Baryonyx** (say bah-ree-on-icks) liked to catch fish with its long and curvy jaw.

FUN FACTS

Did You Know?
Therizinosaurus (say Ther-ra-zy-no-saur-rus) had the biggest dino claws - they grew up to 1 metre long!

T. rex jaws were strong enough to chomp straight through bones.

WOW!

The fastest dino was **Gallimimus** (gall-ee-mee-muss) which could run as fast as a racehorse!

Plant-Munchers

Most dinosaurs were herbivores (plant-eaters) that just loved to guzzle their greens. These eating machines could devour a plant in no time at all.

Diplodocus (say di-plo-doh-kus) swallowed stones to help mash up the tough vegetation it ate.

I think I've chipped a tooth!

Diplodocus's neck was as long as a bus.

All that green matter in the belly brewed up some pretty **nasty farts**. Pardon you, 'Stinkysaurus!'

With its fearsome set of horns, **Triceratops** (say try-sera-tops) was the rhino of its day. Its tough beak could nibble off the best and most juicy plant tips.

FUN FACTS

Hadrosaurus (say had-roh-saw-rus) had nearly 1000 teeth – great for slicing up tough greens.

Stegosaurus wasn't the smartest dinosaur – its brain was only as big as a kitten's.

Meow!

Stegosaurus (say steg-oh-saw-rus) wore its plates in two rows along its back. It might even have been able to change their colour.

Like a giraffe, **Omeisaurus's** (say oh-my-saw-rus) really long neck helped it to reach juicy vegetation on high branches. Oh my!

Iguanodon (say ig-wan-oh-don) walked on all fours, but could stand on its back legs to reach tasty treats.

Apatosaurus (say a-pat-oh-saw-rus) had teeth like blunt pencils that could strip a branch of pine-needles in seconds!

Who goes there?

NO ENTRY

Many herbivore dinosaurs hung out in **herds** to keep them safe from nasty predators like T. rex.

Plant-chewing dinosaurs could eat **100,000 calories** a day - that's the same amount of energy as 1,600 chocolate bars!

WOW!

little and large

Dinosaurs were the biggest land animals that ever lived. The most ground-wobbling giants were the monster herbivores, but lots of dinos were dainty divas.

Teeny **Micropachycephalosaurus** (say my-crow-pak-ee-sef-al-oh-saw-rus) made up for its size with the longest name in the dino world.

Slam dunk!

Anchiornis (say ank-e-or-nis) could fit in the palm of your hand – it was only as tall as a basketball! It used its feathers to glide from tree to tree. Wee!

The biggest eggs in the dino world belonged to **Titanosaurus** (say tie-tan-oh-saw-rus). These ginormous eggs were each as tall as a trumpet!

Quetzalcoatlus (say kwet-za-coh-at-luss) was the world's largest pterosaur (flying reptile). Its wings were as big as a small aeroplane.

The biggest bone ever found belongs to **Seismosaurus** (say size-moh-saw-rus).

Nice to tweet you!

The smallest **pterosaur** (say terr-owe-saw) was no bigger than a sparrow.

'Jumbo-saurus' **Brachiosaurus** (say brak-key-oh-saw-rus) weighed as much as 17 African elephants.

Dino Attack!

Slashing and gnashing their way through the animal kingdom, the bloodthirsty meat-eaters were expert hunters with some dastardly and daring tactics...

Carnivorous (meat-eating) dinosaurs used their cunning camouflage to hide in the undergrowth.

Many meat-eaters had a keen sense of smell. The brain of **T. rex** was roughly the size of three tennis balls and nearly half of this was dedicated to smell!

Bargain buckets on special today!

Deadly **Deinonychus** (say die-non-knee-kus) hunted in numbers, running down its prey just like a wolf-pack.

Do we get a family discount?

FUN FACTS

I have to be very careful wiping my bottom!

One slash from a **Utahraptor's** (say you-tah-rap-tor) 20-cm-long claw could clamp into any tough dino hide, allowing it to use its sharp teeth to kill the prey.

Dino Defense

With so many sharp teeth and claws hiding in bushes and around corners, the peaceful plant-eating dinosaurs needed some clever ways to stay safe and avoid becoming dinner.

Nervous **Ornithomimus** (say or-nith-oh-mee-mus) preferred a quick sprint to take its tasty thighs out of the reach of predators.

Ready...steady...go!

Torosaurus (say tor-oh-saw-rus) rocked the largest head in the dino world and had fearsome horns!

Let's play hide and seek!

Small shrub-nibblers, such as the **Fabrosaurus** (say fab-roh-saw-rus), kept safe by **keeping hidden**!

Size matters! Lots of plant-eating dinosaurs went for pure **bulk**. When you're really chunky, it takes a lot to bring you down.

Travelling as a herd helped keep **Pachyrhinosaurus** (say pack-ee-rye-noh-saw-rus) from harm.

Ankylosaurus (say an-kye-loh-saw-rus) was covered nose to tail in super-tough armour, with a heavy bony club at the end of it!

Maiasaura (say my-oh-saw-rah) protected their nests from egg thieves and were backed up by the rest of the colony.

Did You Know?
Maiasaura's name means 'good mother'...strange if you were a male Maiasaura!

Barosaurus's (say ba-ro-saw-rus) whip-tail was almost as long as eight motorbikes!

WOW!

Stegosaurus tails were sometimes damaged - from battles with other beasties!

Weird and Wonderful

Butting boneheads, big beautiful eyes, flashy crests and foul breath – the dino world had it all!

Hadrosaurus (say had-roh-saw-rus) was part of a group of dinosaurs whose horny beaks looked like they belonged on a very large duck!

This is quackers!

Another hadrosaur, **Saurolophus** (say sore-o-low-fuss), might have had a flap of skin over its nostrils that it could blow up like a balloon. It's party time!

That's cheating!

This knuckleheaded dino called **Colepiocephale** (say co-lep-pee-oh-sef-al-ay) bashed its thick dome-shaped skull together with its mates.

FUN FACTS

Dinosaur-munching super-croc **Sarchosuchus** (say sar-coh-sue-kus) was as long as a truck and weighed as much as eight buffalos. It was super-mean with it too!

Fangs for the lift!

On Wings and Fishy Fin

There were many non-dinosaur reptiles that lived 230-66 million years ago. Some soared in the sky and dived for fish. Others lived beneath the waves like real sea dragons!

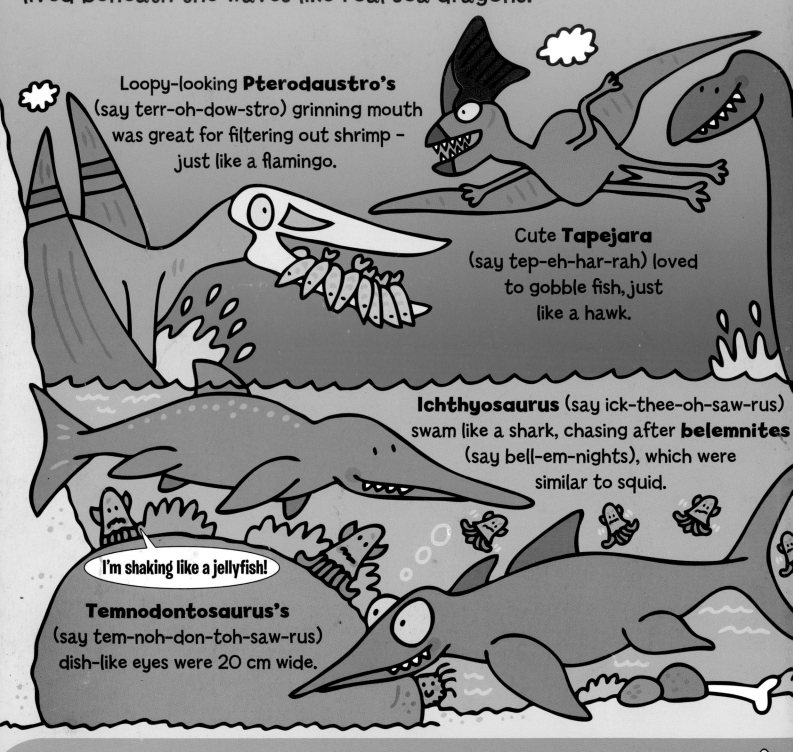

Loopy-looking **Pterodaustro's** (say terr-oh-dow-stro) grinning mouth was great for filtering out shrimp – just like a flamingo.

Cute **Tapejara** (say tep-eh-har-rah) loved to gobble fish, just like a hawk.

Ichthyosaurus (say ick-thee-oh-saw-rus) swam like a shark, chasing after **belemnites** (say bell-em-nights), which were similar to squid.

I'm shaking like a jellyfish!

Temnodontosaurus's (say tem-noh-don-toh-saw-rus) dish-like eyes were 20 cm wide.

FUN FACTS

Some small **pterosaurs** (say terr-oh-sawz) were covered in fur to keep them warm.

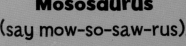

The first swimming reptile fossil ever discovered was **Mososaurus** (say mow-so-saw-rus).

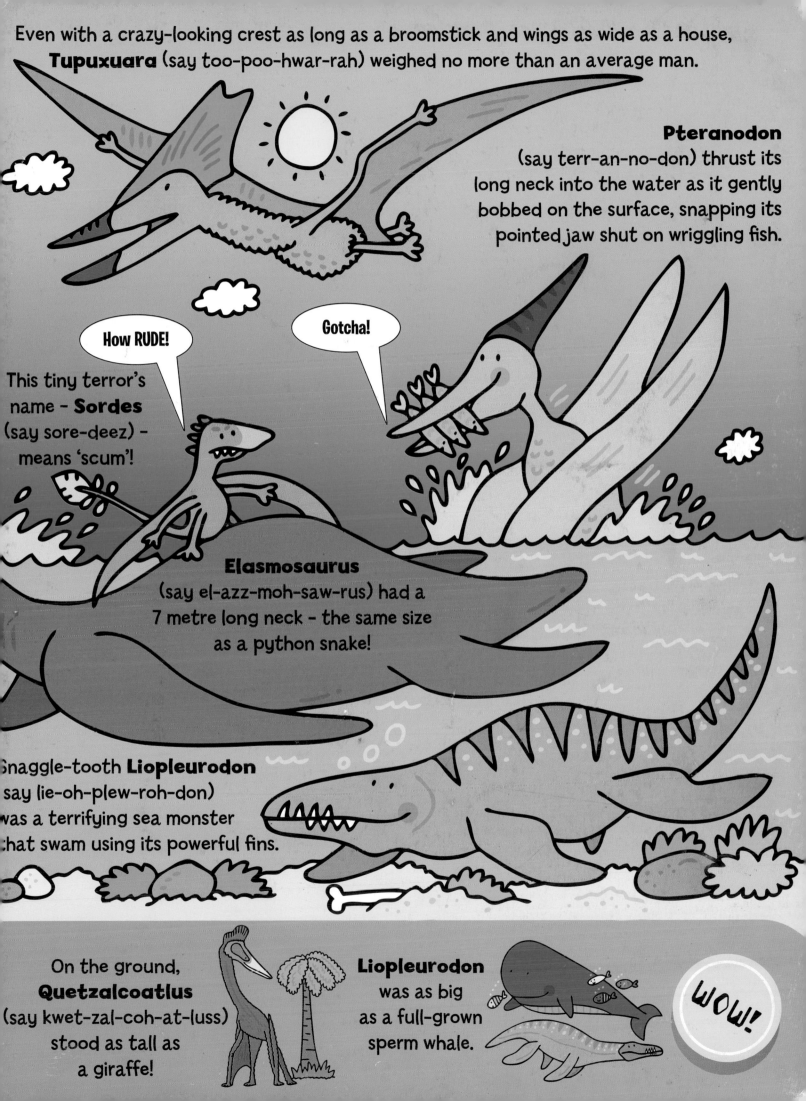

Find out the Dinosaurs

A huge chunk of space rock crashed into Earth 66 million years ago. It was death from outer space and a total disaster for the dinosaurs!

The **comet** that smashed into Earth was made of rock and ice and would have stood taller than Mount Everest!

The giant rock, called a comet, kicked up huge **dust-clouds**, which blocked out the sun for months and caused plants to die.

Vast cracks opened in the planet, with **volcanoes** churning out **lava**, more dust and poisonous clouds.

FUN FACTS

The impact **crater** where the comet hit Earth is in Mexico and is **180–200 km** across.

Rain falling from the clouds was **acidic**, weaker than lemon juice, but enough to affect life.

The world was changing and it spelled the end for the **dinosaurs** and many other plants and animals.

GOODBYE PARTY

As Earth's climate and temperature changed, dinosaurs could no longer survive on the planet.

Food ran low and large dinosaurs went hungry.

Extinct or not? Not all dinosaurs died out – today's birds are descendants of the predatory dinosaurs that survived this global disaster.

Tidal waves caused by the impact would have been hundreds of metres high.

The dino-killing comet was **10-15 kilometres** wide – that would completely cover the city of Edinburgh.

WOW!

Dino Facts

Small-brained chomper **Apatosaurus's** body was 600,000 times bigger than its cat-sized brain.

Nigersaurus (say nye-jer-saw-rus) had the most teeth for a sauropod dino: 500. But it only used 128 of these small shrub-nibbling toothy-pegs at any one time.

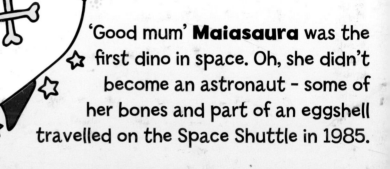

'Good mum' **Maiasaura** was the first dino in space. Oh, she didn't become an astronaut - some of her bones and part of an eggshell travelled on the Space Shuttle in 1985.

One of the largest and most complete **T. rex** skeletons ever found was nicknamed 'Sue'. She lived until she was 28 years old.

The longest near-complete dinosaur skeleton belongs to **Diplodocus**. This maxi-monster was as long as a basketball court.